Who Tells the Crocuses It's Spring?

Who Tells the Crocuses It's Spring?

Favorite Poems
of the Four Seasons

as published in Farm Journal

Compiled by Pearl Patterson Johnson

Illustrations from Original Block Prints by Gwen Frostic
Book Design: Al J. Reagan

COUNTRYSIDE PRESS

a division of Farm Journal, Inc.
Philadelphia, Pennsylvania

Cycle of the Seasons

NATURE lavishes her gifts upon us all—and her appeal through the centuries has been expressed in song, art and verse. But for those who earn their living from the land, Nature's moods have special significance.

Reacting to scenes of their native woods and fields, the authors of these poems put into word pictures the elements of countryside living: the promise of Spring; evolving fulfillment of Summer; garnered treasures of Autumn and, to complete the cycle, the benediction of Winter.

From the hundreds of poems printed in FARM JOURNAL magazine over the past three decades, we share with you 135 of the most representative seasonal verses—all giving evidence of the poets' awareness, humor and reflection.

The illustrations are sensitively created by Gwen Frostic, so well known for her original block prints. They add rare charm to the collection—poems of the four seasons loved by FARM JOURNAL readers who know Nature intimately through their closeness to the earth and its seasonal cycles.

PEARL PATTERSON JOHNSON
Poetry Editor, FARM JOURNAL

CONTENTS

Winter

Winter:
Christmas and New Year

Spring

It's Spring! It's Spring!

Who tells the crocuses it's spring?
What calendar informs the daffodils
To bloom, or notifies the birds to sing,
Or bids the grass to blow across the hills?
What almanac has urged the leaves to wake,
Or stirred the tulips in their narrow beds?
What messenger instructs the buds to break,
Or violets to lift their purple heads?
And yet they know. They know. This is the hour
When spring takes over. Let the winter pass—
You cannot keep it from the wistful flower,
You cannot hide it from the eager grass.
It's spring. It's spring! The news has got around,
Spreading like fire across the quickened ground.

—MAE WINKLER GOODMAN

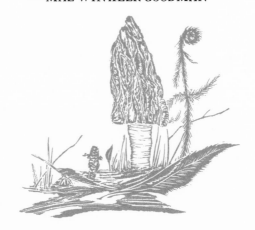

A Red-letter Day

When every budding maple wears
On every twig a gilded locket,
When ponds are loud with clicking frogs
Like marbles in a small boy's pocket,

When well-bred goldfinches ignore
The ribaldries that bluejays utter
At picnics where the grass is spread
With dandelion pats of butter,

Then you may ring the calendar
With scarlet, though it shine or rain,
And run outside without your gloves,
For April has come true again.

—YETZA GILLESPIE

Spring House Cleaning

I'm short of breath, my heart beats fast
When nature is a-greening;
I'll bet you think that I'm in love—
It's just from spring house cleaning.

—BLANCHE A. HJERPE

Dawdling Winter

This backward spring reminds me of the way
The children used to think of everything
At bedtime—any quick excuse to play
Another hour: the drinks—remembering
Small joys they had not told—prolonged good-nights—
Good-night, good-night, again, again, again.
Closing the door and turning out the lights
Was never final as it should have been.
A coyote, wind, a cricket's harmless noise
Was cause to fret, and I had not the heart
To chasten them. Now winter time enjoys
Playing a similar, slow counterpart:
    Reluctantly still dawdling in the snow
    Long past the hour for frosty days to go.

—MERYLE MOORE SIMPSON

Nature's Workshop

The wind is strumming muted chords
On orchard boughs of peach and pear.
The sun is raining golden beams,
And petals scurry everywhere.

The busy robin trills and chirps
As he unravels worms all day.
How Nature's magic needles hum!
The earth is busy stitching May.

—ANNE BONNER MARLEY

Spring Ritual

Today I saw an act of faith:
A man was on his knees,
Not in a pew, but by a fence
Planting apple trees.

—SUDIE STUART HAGER

Song Sparrow

In February, he began
A brave campaign to shake
The slumber from the apple tree;
To sing it wide awake.
In March, his voice was loud despite
The wind hawk's threatening.
He clung to his small, barren twig
And trilled his faith in spring.
But now, with April here at last,
His song becomes a shout
Of triumph, as it spurs the buds
And drives the blossoms out!

—VIRGINIA MORAN EVANS

Winds of March

The wind leapfrogs and somersaults,
And then slides down
A winter-polished hill of white;
Tickles a tree, then recklessly vaults
To waken a sleeping town
By helping dawn push away the night.
Oh, such a wind as this will bring
A rush of tiny miracles called Spring.

—EILEEN BRANSON

Spring Sunset

The redbud trees' reflections make
Pink pools of color in the lake.
The sky has copied them, and glows
With delicate and dimming rose.
A distant hill has, settled on it,
A soft pink cloud for an Easter bonnet.

—MILDRED GOFF

Faith of a Farmer

A farmer understands deep certainties,
Knows winter is a doorway to the spring,
Walks quiet aisles of prayer where templed trees
Prove death a season for each living thing.
He turns fresh furrows to the sun each year
And feels new sunlight on his old, old fields;
Each drop of dew and rain that touches here
Will bring him hope for plenteous harvest yields.
He bares his head against an April sky,
Sure of the constant greening of the grass;
When seedlings sprout he does not question why;
Hears trust in wild geese calling as they pass.
His faith affirms the resurrection claim
When spring returns a green and living flame.

—HELEN VIRDEN

Reassurance

If I need reassurance now,
With snow piled high
Outside my door,
That spring will come once more,
I need but to descend
My cellar stair.
The very breath of spring
Is captured there
In row on row of crystal jars . . .
The bright procession led
By early May garbed in strawberry red,
Followed by June, resplendent
In a gown of soft pea-green,
As lovely as you've ever seen
And trooping after
Bright with amber laughter,
Are all the golden summer hours,
As fresh and colorful as flowers,
Oh, yes, my cellar shelves impart
Promise rich enough to satisfy
The need of any doubting heart

—MYRTLE VORST SHEPPARD

The Shrew

The wind was out of sorts today.
The wind was like a shrew
Whose anger fed upon itself,
As anger will, and grew
Until, at fever pitch and crazed,
She smashed the wanton rose
And banged at every captious gate
And snatched at hanging clothes.
She shrieked with high emotion as
She slapped the wayward brook,
While skittish clouds in terror wept,
And mighty oak trees shook.

Tonight, at last, her wrath is spent.
Exhausted, she reclines
Upon the mourner's bench and croons
Apologetic lines.

—ELIANA BEAM

Farm Boy's Dream

Last night, lying here in these barracks, I
dreamed that I heard again the pigeons coo
softly as they serenely walked the ridge-pole
on the dairy barn back home.

I heard the hungry squealing of a litter of
pigs as they followed their mother about.

I heard in the distance the clank of milk cans
and the roar of a motor as the milk truck squeezed
slowly through the spring mud of a barn lot.

I heard the sharp plunk as one of the perch in our
stock watering tank brought down another fly.

I heard the whistling of my brother and the bark
of our collie as they took the cows to the new pasture.

I heard the swish of the barn swallows as
they dive-bombed a cat in the barn loft.

I heard the helpless plea of a lamb when he
awoke from his siesta and found his mother
gone—and the answering bleat of his mother.

I faintly heard the regular clicks of the corn
planter and the decisive "whoa" of the hired man
as the team reached the end of another row.

I heard the shrill squeak of the weather-
vane as the wind changed slightly.

I heard the rattle of harness chains and the
soothing voice of my father.

I heard the lonely call of a crow.

I heard the monotonous hum of a tractor.

I heard the soft cheeping of chicks in the
brooder house.

I heard the thousand and one things that
make our farm my home.

MELVIN E. WEST

Of Hunger

Come till the soil for seed . . .
Fulfill the urgent need
Of fare, from fallow lands.

Soil holds the pulse of birth . . .
Come, scatter grain
Upon the earth,
That no wan child reach out
In vain, imploring hands.

—MILDRED CARTWRIGHT JOBSON

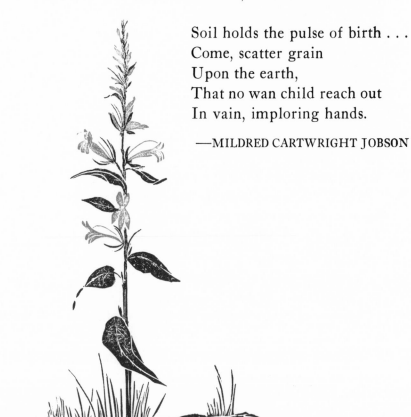

Old Garden

She planted hollyhocks along the wall,
A lilac bush beside the garden gate,
A rambler rose that climbed so straight and tall,
The arbor is unequal to the weight.
And so it sags a little on one end,
As tired shoulders droop sometimes at night.
Amid the waste of weeds, the colors blend
Into an earthly rainbow of delight.

The little house she lived in then is gone,
For time has worked its elemental way,
The chimney stones lie on the grassless lawn,
Like mouldering bones returning to the clay.
But beauty that she planted still flames here,
A monument the earth rebuilds each year.

—CATHERINE E. BERRY

To a Tidy Housewife

You've said that the arbutus
Is your favorite of all
Spring's careless wealth of flowers,
Since its petals seldom fall.
Accept then this arbutus
So delicately sweet,
Causing no disorder
For you who are so neat.
But—don't forget the places
Thick with leaf-mould where it's found—
It had surely died of frostbite
Had some trim one raked that ground.

—VIOLET ALLEYN STOREY

Precaution

April's lawn will take no chance
With winter's flight, and spring's advance;
She buttons up her new green coat
With dandelions to the throat.

—ISABEL M. WOOD

Bloodroot

Winter lingers—in our thoughts, despair
Lies like a stone; our hearts are cold
Like snow on bleak fields everywhere
When winter is old.

Through last-year leaves there springs a flower
Which seems to say, "Have you not known
That deathless love which has the power
To melt the snow, to roll away the stone?"

—ANNE BRADLEY

Frolic of the Rain

Rain
Falling since morning,
Dripping from barn roof,
Gossiping in gutters,
Sliding down new leaves.
By evening you are gone—
All but one leftover puddle
Holding the last light of day.

—JANE LINDSTROM

To My Son's First Teachers

Let the spring colt run free,
At least a little longer.

Now, while the new sun warms his soul
Until it melts into silvery streams of laughter;

Now, while the south wind catches his whistle
And spills it out in golden daffodils of joy.

While his heart knows only loving
And his legs want only running
Let him have a wide, wide meadow.
At least a little longer.

He'll have much time in harness later on.
Let the spring colt run free.

—GENE LOGSDON

Rebirth

Each spring a million daffodils
Break through the frost-sealed earth,
As if God wrote in flower gold
The message of rebirth.

—PEARL PATTERSON JOHNSON

Tomboy Spring

I like a tomboy spring, bright-haired and bold,
Whose merry glances tease away the cold,
Whose warm lips kiss the daffodils awake,
Whose slim hands ruffle up each sleeping lake,
Who impudently whistles home the birds
And coaxes trees with green, enchanting words . . .
I like a gamin spring who gayly flirts
Down country lanes in apple-blossom skirts!

—GERALDINE ROSS

Spring Invasion

I shall have lilacs now as Spring advances;
They will capture the city, street by street,
Proud behind plate-glass in the florists' windows,
Crowding the curb where the lines of traffic meet.

Then, as the dusk descending over the roof-tops
Pales underneath the city's brilliant night,
I shall recall the scent of a country garden,
I shall remember the gleam of a neighbor's light.

—BEULAH RIDGEWAY WINANS

Spring Performance

God has taken the winter reel
Of black and white days
Off the projector of time
And fastened into position
His beautiful technicolor feature—
The magic film of Spring.

—ESTELLE FINNEGAN

28

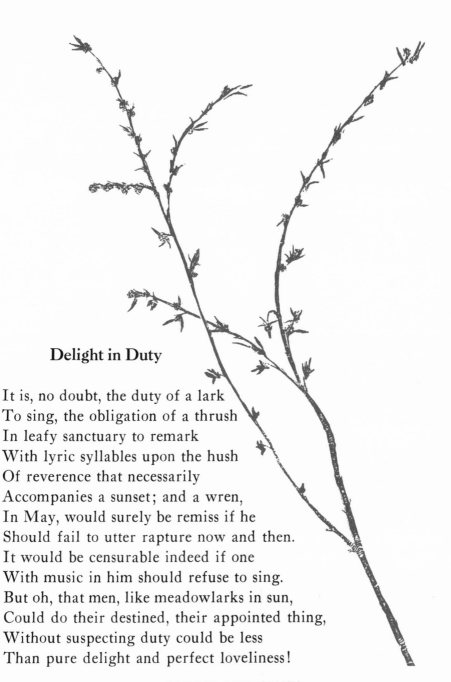

Delight in Duty

It is, no doubt, the duty of a lark
To sing, the obligation of a thrush
In leafy sanctuary to remark
With lyric syllables upon the hush
Of reverence that necessarily
Accompanies a sunset; and a wren,
In May, would surely be remiss if he
Should fail to utter rapture now and then.
It would be censurable indeed if one
With music in him should refuse to sing.
But oh, that men, like meadowlarks in sun,
Could do their destined, their appointed thing,
Without suspecting duty could be less
Than pure delight and perfect loveliness!

—JANE H. MERCHANT

Forsythia

April came dancing down the lane,
A roguish twinkle in her eyes;
She waved her wand, and magic rain
Showered bare boughs outside my pane
With hosts of golden butterflies.

—GERTRUDE PERRY STANTON

Tomorrow Will Be April

Tomorrow will be April;
In the air tonight
Smell the poignant promise
Of the spring's delight.

Harken to the signal
From the marshy land,
Clear and pregnant message
Of the peeper-band.

And the young moon pointing
Just above the trees—
April comes tomorrow:
Smell it on the breeze.

—ALMA ROBERTS GIORDAN

30

Adolescent

April is a long-limbed child
Whose growth exceeds her gowns,
Bursting out at all the seams
Of winter's hand-me-downs.

—JAN DAWSON JENSEN

Spring Song

Had God no other way to speak
His love than through a budding tree,
No syllables but those now hung
Along these branches, this to me
Would be all Heaven in a song
As clear as that of any bird:
All paradise framed in a leaf
Shaped to His promise like a word
Emerald enameled, and
Fresh and lovely from His hand.

—ELEANOR ALLETTA CHAFFEE

Psalm of the Homemaker

Hear me, the Homemaker,
Hark to my song.
Call me "the Homemaker."
My day is long.
It is filled with a round of tasks, each trivial in itself,
yet the sum of my labor makes possible the progress
of the world.
My rest is sacrificed willingly to meet the needs of
my loved ones.
I seek neither shorter hours nor more pay.
When circumstance demands, I know a twenty-four
hour working day.
I belong to no union save the Unselfed Order of
Mother Love!
When the welfare of my young seems at stake, I do
not hesitate—
I enter the arena—mind, soul, and ballot.
And yet I realize—and teach my brood—that Love,
Harmony, and Unity are the strength of nations, as
well as the keystones of happy family life.
Though I give my body to the treadmill of toil, my
mind reaches sensitive fingers into the future, con-
stantly moving the pawns of life to play a winning
game.

The development of each child into a sane and useful citizen is the stake for which I play.

I give my body to be broken, and gladly go down into the Valley of the Shadow, that I may bring new life into this world.

Lacking me, there would be neither merchant, nor farmer, neither doctor nor lawyer, neither statesman nor scientist.

Lacking me, man would cease to exist.

I am the heart of life.

I am the mainspring of the universe.

Call me the "Homemaker."

—MARION HENDRICK RAY

Between Seasons

Reflected like a double death, our tree
Filled the rain pool to the black-branched brim,
And we who walked in this cold interim
Wondered at life's slow sterility.
When you had gone, I waited quietly
Within a house long locked to April's whim.
I felt the raindrops stream and join again,
Rain down the windows; down the heart of me.

But now, after a cool blue wash of sleep
Forsythia bells, too hurried for small leaf,
Tap their blooms against my window pane;
Staccato blackbirds come back to explain
It's Spring! Life and the season, I have found
Are swelling with the burst of yellow sound.

—JEANETTE HINDS

Where Children Are . . .

Let me be where children are:
I'll never miss a cloud or star,
Never miss a stone or flower
If I am with them one small hour.
Let me be where children play
For laughter surely runs that way.
Let me be where children sing
For there is God's eternal Spring.

—RUBY ZAGOREN

Budget Beater

In Spring the thought occurs to me:
How very lovely it would be,
If I, like lilac tree, or rose,
Could *grow* my Easter hat and clothes.

—MARY SHIRK

Great Moment

I turned a page, and suddenly
Winter fell away from me;
My eyes grew wonder-filled to find
The dark walls 'round me all entwined
With morning glories' glowing red;
Pink hollyhocks leaned overhead.
I breathed the spice of marigold,
Watched soft petunia buds unfold,
I touched the silk of four o'clocks,
Smiled into winking eyes of phlox.

Lost is the winter's venomed tongue,
The world and I again are young,
Forgotten snow and sleet and hail—
Seed catalogs are in the mail!

—BARBARA OVERTON CHRISTIE

Spring Morning

Now March has tossed the snowy covers back,
And April
Plucks at the sleeping Earth
With soft, warm fingers, calling:
"Get up! Get up! You have a date
With flower-laden May!"

—LYLE W. THOMAS

Brook in April

The little brook is a silver ribbon
Left from the holidays,
That Spring has found and used to tie
About her first bouquets.

—MARION DOYLE

Spring Campaign

Above the sweet, young green of clover leaves,
The sky that was so blue puts on a veil
Of gray. A sudden rain-burst comes and weaves
Across the fragrant meadows, then, a gale
Of strong south wind goes prancing past.
The farmer, looking upward, nods and smiles.
Rich promise lurks in heavens overcast!
Then, suddenly, green fields, and trees, and stiles,
The heavens, and dark, new furrows, blend
With silver rain in wild confusion. All
The teeming earth and pouring heavens send
Their forces out at some great battle call.
At last, earth's green offensive has begun!
She routs gray winter with her rain and sun!

—LOIS KINGSLEY PELTON

Hope

What is hope but another word for April?
A symbol of fresh growth? The gallant blade
As it breaks through the ground of a frosty spirit?
A bough launching new leaves in a windy glade?
What is hope but the bright buds of courage
Substituting rose for the winter's pallor?
Crying to the tired heart: "We will triumph!"
What is hope but the foliage of valor
Floating on sun-bright air; a banner unfurled,
Silken and rich and green on a waking world?

—PAULINE HAVARD

38

Green Gardener

The neighbors say my thumb is green,
And I would furthermore disclose
That I've the greenest knees in town,
And also lovely grass-stained hose.

—LENORE EVERSOLE FISHER

Sonnet for Gardeners

I think that we who tend the growing things
Grow too; our spirits feel akin to birds,
And lift far out on sudden, urgent wings
To skim with them and speak their airy words.
I cannot nurture trees (from saplings grown)
And see them rising skyward with such pride
Without a tiptoe feeling of my own,
As though we reached together, side by side.
And as I tend my garden, bright with flowers,
And pull the tares and plant anew the seeds.
I, too, am blessed with rain, with sunny hours,
With all the bloom my hungry spirit needs.
We, deeply rooted too in living earth,
Move close to God with every plant's new birth.

—ELIZABETH TERRYL

Storm Dragon

It crouches in the northwest;
Black, its yellow eyes gleaming.
All live things which can run scurry to safety,
While trees shiver and cower.
Suddenly, with a roar, it pounces,
Rending branch and flower in its path.
Its fury satisfied
With beating to earth each hapless petal,
And leaving great trees with drooping arms,
It passes by, snarls diminishing
In the distance. For a moment, changing course,
It lifts a clawed foot and hesitates
Before Nature glances over her shoulder
At the storm's broad rounded back,
Shakes herself,
And the first song-sparrow sings.

—ISABEL M. WOOD

Rain in the Wood

I like to think how glad a forest is
For rain it had been needing! Surely each
Furred creature loves the smell of it at his
Small doorway, sniffing it, just out of reach
Of its cool touch; and every inhabitant
Of a woodland must delight to hear the sound
Of rain on tree and underbrush and plant,
With all the myriad tricklings to the ground.
And sometimes, walking in a rainy wood,
I seem to hear the thirsty leaves above
My pathway whispering their gratitude—
While here and there a bird sings out its love
Of rain—and, as before a banquet spread,
The very forest seems to bow its head.

—ELAINE V. EMANS

Psalm of Springtime

"The willow tree is dead,"
the woman said. "For weeks now
I've been waiting, and still I cannot
see one sign of green. You'd better
cut it down and throw it
on the burning pile."
  The man's hoe rose and fell,
  as though he hadn't heard.
  She fussed,
"You know it's dead—probably last summer's
drought brought it about. But,"
wistfully, "I did think, having grown
so tall, it would survive this hillside . . .
  Yet I suppose a willow only thrives
  beside a stream where, as the seasons
  pass, its twigs float far away
  to root in other pleasant places.
   I'll miss it, though—its
   golden wands against the winter skies.
   And then, first thing to come alive again—
   fountaining a Psalm of springtime
   over the garden.

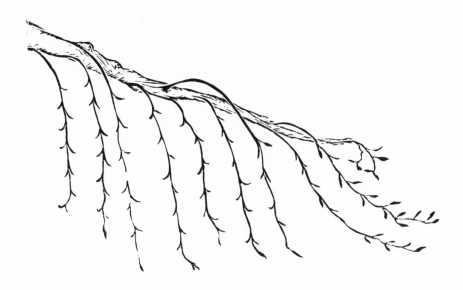

But now, it's surely dead. Just chop
it off, right to the ground.
I hate to have it standing there so bare.
You will remember, won't you?

*Have you seen? Have you seen
the willow?
It is green.* Little buds
are coming out, all up the trunk.
And a topmost branch has leaves.
How fortunate you never got around to taking it away.
One can never really know, can one, how deep a willow
root may go."

—JANE CARTER

Shape of the Wind

Who says the wind is shapeless
Has never seen the sea
When wind, as shell-shaped waves disguised,
Sculptures immensity.

    And he has not beheld, in fact,
    A wealth of soft blond curls
    On wild March days, stretched out like silk
    From the heads of little girls.

The one red leaf in autumn,
That navigates the blue
Thin air, is but a tiny ship
With only wind for crew.

    And whether bare trees quiver
    Or ferns bend in the shade,
    The wind in all these many forms
    Is here in masquerade.

—HARRIET GRAY BLACKWELL

Spring Storm

The hounds of wind went keening through my garden,
The clouds leaned down to set their torrents free,
Buffeting three lonely wild birds flying,
Beating down new grass and twisting every tree.

The wind-hounds passed, the dark clouds broke and shifted,
Showing mosaic bits of blue between,
And rain that sequined my cherry tree with silver
Left crystal cross-stitch patterns on my window screen.

—ALMA ROBISON HIGBEE

Summer

Across the Years

Ah, lost sweet summer, windy hills and hollows,
Wide lonesome fields where flaming hawkweeds grew;
Clear skies of June laced with the flight of swallows;
Ah, shadowy hay-sweet barn that once he knew;
House by an orchard where the harvest apples
Ripened and tumbled in the sunny grass:
I must go back and back to where the dapples
Of sun and shadow flicker as they pass
Across your window sills. House, do your floors
Laugh with the dancing feet of children now?
Barn, do the swallows nest above your doors?
Is hay piled fragrant in your dusty mow?
I must go back across the years and find
The dream of peace that lingers in my mind.

—LEONA AMES HILL

In an Orchard

Deep in an orchard, silence never reigns;
  On every bough there's the sound of dancing feet
When music that the wind brings stirs the veins
  Of restless leaves, green slippered, summer-fleet—
Soft sounds of motion, fairy-faint yet real.
  A twig snaps, or a small woodpecker's bill
Taps at the door beyond which lies his meal.
  Frail moth wings beat the air, strange insects spill
Their song and laughter, loves and hates and fears,
  For one who listens with undeafened ears.

                  —LALIA MITCHELL THORNTON

Rain after Drouth

A little while ago the fields were dust:
The meager blades of corn stood withering;
The spindling stalks of grain were brown as crust.
The sultry air discouraged flight of wing.
An arm of thunder bumped against the hill;
The sun drew sullenly behind a cloud,
While brooding trees, like statues, waited, still;
And breathing seemed extravagantly loud.

I heard the first faint sound of rushing rain
Against the hill's green host of thirsty leaves!
I saw the great drops lift the dust, and stain
The road, and gather on the porch's eaves!
And from his bough, a thrush was moved to song—
A lyric burst of gladness, free and strong!

—WEBB DYCUS

Boy Beside a Stream

Beside the brook, tall cat-tails make a screen,
A lark flies up—his gay song fills the sky;
And, Indian-quiet, here, the boy has knelt to lean
Above the water, watching the dragon fly
Skate, then zoom through bowered space.
A whirlpool of bubbles starts
From turtle shallows, where green lace
Reflected from the trees is pierced with sunlight darts.
Of milkweed pods the boy makes silvery boats,
And launches the little fleet upon the stream,
Each bearing down the current, as it floats,
His young and eager dream.

—ALMA ROBISON HIGBEE

Magic Country

The magic country of a child
Is wide and green and sweet
From wild-rose scent and clover-bloom
In hazy summer heat.
　　Grass-blades are a forest there;
　　Ladybirds are people;
　　Bees are belfry-men who ring
　　The lupins' golden steeple.

While surely in that childhood-world
The Giant, Time, stands still,
Bewitched by what he sees and hears
Across that curving hill—
　　Children playing make-believe
　　In a cool maple's shadow;
　　Safe in the flower-printed lap
　　Of some old, kindly meadow.

—PAULINE HAVARD

Roots

"You plant them early in July," she told me,
The son who didn't know the pleasures of the old days.
"Come February, the frost will take out all the bitterness—
Fixed right, they make the first good eating of the year."

So I planted parsnips and planned, come February,
To take them to her to fix right, for who else could?
We'd eat them together, relishing old-fashioned ways
That meant nothing except to our kind.

But February did not come for her, just November
With a cruel coldness that was not the weather only,
That was the weather least of all.
The greentops of the parsnips fell and died—their time.

A pile of leaves now rests within my garden,
Beneath which parsnip roots lie snug against the cold.
I stand and stare today, too long, at that low mound.
It looks like Mamma's grave.

A last and tenuous link between her soul and mine,
Between old days dying and new ones yet to live,
Between an old woman saying goodby
And a young man, taking root.

But who will cook those parsnips, come February,
Who will eat them, relishing rich old ways?
And will the frost, by then,
Take out the bitterness?

—GENE LOGSDON

Sweet Peas

Awhile they rest here,
Fluttering on their stems
Like butterflies in summer.
Their silk wings glow
With delicate hues—
Blue and purple
And pale lemon.
Some are streaked with rose and cherry,
Others gleam like opals,
These, silver luster of high moon.
Small wonder we expect
To see them taking flight.

—MARION DOYLE

The Drouth Breaking

The southwest wind had punished the plains all day.
The papery corn-blades rattled with every gust,
Dry and wilted. The scoured fields flowed with dust.
Grasshoppers, rising from stubble, hurtled away.
The wind died out near sunset. Clouds, blue-gray
And rimmed on each fore-edge with a silver crust,
Piled up northwestward—smoke-dark and smeared with rust
In the farther distance. Lightning began to play
Silently in the masses. Slowly they mounted,
Hid the horizon; the circlets swelled and spread
Solid across the sky, weighing the air.
The early stars, while they could still be counted,
Dimmed, went out. Suddenly, overhead,
The tension broke. Sweet rain was everywhere!

—ELIJAH L. JACOBS

Clover Field

Nothing is lovelier than tangled clover
When rain falls gently on the purple field;
Nothing so fragrant as the breath of blossoms
Foretelling the reward that they will yield.

Nothing is restful as a field of clover
Where drowsy, summer bees go velvet-shod;
Nothing so peaceful as these sloping acres
That bear the purple signature of God.

—OMA CARLYLE ANDERSON

July's My Darling

July's my darling! July is my plum!
July's the promise of harvests to come.

July's brooks cool me; her minnows bite.
July's corn stretches and snaps in the night.

July's the red, white, and blue on a pole,
July's long evenings are good for my soul.

—ROBERT D. MCMILLEN

August

I know no month that I love
More than August.
I know no month that holds
A greater treasure store,
With sunshine spread like melted
Butter on every valley floor,
And kittens wrapped in velvet slumber
Beside my kitchen door.
I know no sweeter, happier time
Than tranquil, lazy August
When clusters of yellow butterflies
Scallop the winding roadway's dust,
And aimless clouds, fluffy and high,
Like cottony circus candy,
Drift across the deep blue sky!

—MYRTLE VORST SHEPPARD

Child and Brook

Today my child has known a brook.
At first she stood with probing toe
Thrust and withdrawn, with intent
Eager but fearful. Then slow
Delight possessed her. The chill
Spray feathered her ankles, the swift
Water sang past her feet; in still
Warm shallows she watched the drift
Of bubbled foam, saw skippers dart.
She stroked the stones, felt ripples play.
Later she'll hold this hour apart
Remembering this brook today.

—ELIZABETH ANDERSON

Boy Fishing

For hours he has sat beside the stream,
Bathed by the sun, and in reflective eyes
The radiance of morning-glory skies
Holding the moment gathered in his dream.

The rod grows from his hands; here is no wish
For anything beyond this golden hour
That opens slowly, like a folded flower.
Incidental is the bait, the fish.

He watches minnows trace a silver track
Beyond the mud that oozes through his toes.
He reaches for his shoes at the day's close;
The sun a bright medallion on his back.

Then, gathering his line, he will depart,
Two tiny sunfish his apparent gain;
Yet all the years ahead may not contain
The dreams that he has reeled into his heart.

—MAE WINKLER GOODMAN

Summer Night

Untroubled clouds drift high above the plain,
A yellow moon sifts down a powdery light
Upon the miles on miles of growing grain.
These are the hours when deep silences reign.
Here is no echo of the rolling drum,
Yet our next neighbor's boy has gone to fight
And my one sister knits at night
Her face too white
Save for a glow of rose when letters come.
I know that skies can fall and letters cease
Although, out here, great stars look down in peace.
But in this quiet, broken only by the sound
Of some small creature stirring on the ground,
I feel a certainty that mankind will
Return again to love the fertile field
And seek no further wealth than this:
A yellow moon, a light wind's kiss,
A stretch of ripening wheat, starlit and still,
And at the summer's end a golden yield.

—PRUDENCE K. GEAREY

Obvious Truth

To send a small boy with a grocery list
Tucked in his pocket, is to court disaster.
Summer teases, and tugs at his wrist,
Calling his name, and urging, "Faster!
I have a stone wall here for you to climb;
Whose are the tracks that curve here through the clover?
Let the errand go—later there will be time;
Here is a hedge I think you can jump over."

To summon a small boy, knee-deep in July,
For any useful errand is to assert
The power of Jupiter—to cleave his sky
With bolts of lightning, leaving him unhurt,
But vanquished nonetheless, unwilling slave,
Stripped of the transient joys that freedom gave.

—ELEANOR ALLETTA CHAFFEE

Late Summer

The last of summer comes. These are the days
Of dreamy beauty, when, in woodland lanes,
And sun-burned fields, a thin, blue evil of haze
Appears. With gusty music, now, swift rains
Run through the old, brown corn, and streaks of gold
On leaves are autumn's messages. Now, too,
The aster's royal purple stands up bold
By farm-yard fences, and the wind goes through
The orchard, singing hoarsely. There, we feel
A rich, expectant sense of wealth to come!
The bees have felt it, too. They dive and reel
Around the fruit and raise a constant hum.
The last of summer—and, from kitchen doors,
A smell of fragrant jam and bread-dough pours.

—LOIS KINGSLEY PELTON

Noon

The droning hum of farm machinery
For awhile is done.
The corn bends slightly downward
Relaxing in the sun.

Under the mulberry trees
The cows stand idly by,
Unmindful of the cotton clouds
That float through the larkspur sky.

The windmill grinds to a whirring stop,
The fan points to the west.
It is high noon in the country
And the whole farm stops to rest.

—MARJORIE RICHARDSON PHELPS

August Promise

There is a fragrance and a music here,
A song of harvest: each drop is a note
Of plentitude, the perfume is a sheer
Enjoyment of the apple in the throat.
One tastes the rain here; not just bits of wet
Upon the lips, but all that soon will fill
The barns and bins and cool, dark cellars.
Let the faint tune play itself against the sill,
The windows stream low melody, the lawn
Lift up each blade to hear till sound is gone.

—GERALDINE ROSS

Picking Wild Blackberries

As my bucket fills, so my cup
Of content is brimming up.

Brook water sings; mint is sweet;
Dust motes sparkle in the heat.

A cowbell tinkles, bees drone by;
A hawk sails down a gentian sky.

Clouds trail shadows, blue and still,
On the summit of a hill.

If fingers and if lips are stained,
Consider what the heart has gained.

—ETHEL ROMIG FULLER

Farewell Summer

Acre on acre, mile on mile,
    Like spray from a waterfall,
The little wild white asters
    Offer their beauty for all:
Fairyland-flowers that frost
    Will copy on window panes;
Blossoms, like breath of winter,
    Drifting the valleys and plains.

When the wind passes they whisper,
    Like the sound of the sea in a shell,
A silver good-bye to summer:
    Summer, farewell . . . farewell . . .

—MARION DOYLE

Autumn

My Mind, in Autumn

Always the autumn turns my mind aside
From any thought of mediocrity.
It is as if the haze, in purple tide,
The burnished copper curves of a tall tree,
Were much too wonderful for me to know,
Yet they are at my finger tips, my hand.
I need not question scarlet winds that blow
Across my tawny pastures, down my land,
Nor curling petals of chrysanthemums,
Planted in childhood days to edge our porch,
Nor the gold beech on which a red-head drums,
Nor asters, nor the goldenrod's quick torch.
I only need deny the commonplace,
And know, with certainty, my Father's grace.

—ANOBEL ARMOUR

The Common Road

Here is so much beauty, though the trees
Stand bare against the pale November sky,
Empty of leaves and birds, and all the flowers
Are dead, and the grass is brown and dry.

    Here is beauty in the quiet winding road
    That leads toward home beneath the forest tree,
    In shadows that lie long across the land,
    Tracing the afternoon's tranquility;

In seed pod patterns, exquisite as lace,
In graceful grass that bends beside the stone,
In milkweed's gold-lined purses, open now,
From which the powder puffs were lately blown.

    Here is so much of beauty! But the heart
    Must search it out before the eye can see.
    Here is delight beside the common road,
    For here we journey with the Deity!

—EVADNE SCOTT BEEBE

Indian Summer

A briefly undetermined season caught
Between the moods of warmth and chilling frost
Unfolds a view of summer's afterthought,
Of looking back for treasures lately lost.
A wistful hush is spread across the field
As nature speaks in solemn muted tone,
Expectant, fearful, creatures wait to yield
To forces strangely sensed and yet unknown.

Subdued and deep, the slanting shadows weave
A benediction holding fond farewell,
A requiem of summer taking leave,
A slow surrender tuned to autumn's spell.
The bolder seasons dare not to intrude
Upon this gentle, pensive interlude.

—FLORENCE JANSSON

Question for the First Day of School

Time again for erasers and tablets—remember?
Some hearts must skip backward, while young feet skip on.
Why is it the loudest footsteps, each September,
Are those of the children who have grown up and gone?

—MINNIE HITE MOODY

Red Mittens

At eight, I send my children off to school,
Bundled against the cold in scarlet wool;
   All day, I watch bright leaves from oak trees fly,
And see red mittened hands that waved goodbye.

—ANNE BRADLEY

A Wish for Autumn

When Autumn lifts her copper urn
And tips it up to pour out gold
Over the leaves, when brown trees turn
To crimson as the year grows old,
May there be days of warmth and song
When Indian Summer smiles and walks
Where goldenrod, erect and strong
Burns yellow flames on umber stalks.
May there be days as rich and mellow
As Summer's; may a last bird sing
To tremble leaves that have turned yellow,
To keep the heart young till the Spring!

—PAULINE HAVARD

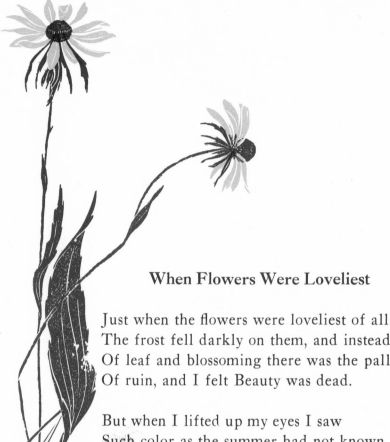

When Flowers Were Loveliest

Just when the flowers were loveliest of all
The frost fell darkly on them, and instead
Of leaf and blossoming there was the pall
Of ruin, and I felt Beauty was dead.

But when I lifted up my eyes I saw
Such color as the summer had not known,
And my heart was filled with joy and awe
As earth in autumn's gallant splendor shone.

Then that was gone, and all the world was drear
And graceless, till last night the white surprise
Of snow came whispering down. Now sunshine spills
A glory past all dreaming from the clear
Tall sky, till I can bear no more. My eyes
Are blinded by the beauty on the hills.

—CLARA AIKEN SPEER

Autumn Twilight

Sunset with all its flame of gold and red
Has slowly turned to softer shades; a light
Wind stirs the leaves on trees that have held tight.
The horses whinner, anxious to be fed
Their oats and clover hay; high overhead
The first pale stars pin-prick the azure height;
A dog's bark breaks the barnyard drone of night
Anticipating meal of milk and bread.
The pastel colors die out of the west;
The pasture twinkles with the glowing fly
Where bullfrogs croak. The soft moon-rays are dim
As darkness spreads her slumber robe for rest.
The farmer lifts his eyes up to the sky
In awe at mysteries beyond earth's rim.

—EMMA THOMAS SCOVILLE

One Day for Thanks

One day for giving thanks; and yet the sun
Sends abundant reassurance with each ray
Through all the year, and seed selects no one
Day's interval for growing want away
From earth; there is no stipulated hour
Alone of one brief season, when eyes may see
The intricate, slow opening of a flower
And the long rhythms of a wind-blown tree.
And since there are no set, specific times
When birds wake sudden music from still air
And children's lilting laughter soars and climbs,
How shall we set a time for thankful prayer?
How shall we pay, in one short interlude,
Our year-long debt of joyous gratitude?

—JANE H. MERCHANT

October Secret

The blue of rain-washed skies could never match
The blueness of his eyes that sunny day,
When his mother said that he might plant a patch
Of pumpkins at the garden's farthest way,
If he would water them and watch them grow
And keep the weeds out with his little hoe.

The wisdom of six green summers companioned him
Down the rows, and though his mother spoke of pies
Golden brown and crimped, and crusty at the rim,
A secret crinkled up the small boy's eyes.
For he saw jack-o'-lanterns in the vines of green
And goblins for a splendid Hallowe'en.

—ALMA ROBISON HIGBEE

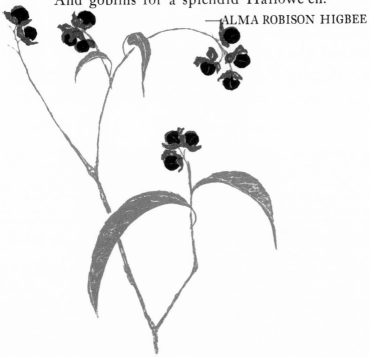

77

October Morning

Last night October lit the torches
    Of the sumac trees
To light her way through the moonless wood,
    Unmindful of the breeze.
Now, see the landscape all afire—
    Leaf-tongues of flame
Licking maple and briar,
    While meadows and hillsides,
Fanned by her cloak,
    Go up in a cloud of wild aster smoke.

—MARION DOYLE

Portrait in an Old Mirror

This is the room I slept in when a child:
Four-poster bed, the china shepherdess
Forever by her china love beguiled;
The cross-stitch motto asking God to bless
This house (and her who made it long away).
This is the room I wake in: this same sun
Poured out its gold upon another day
Whose sand through Time's dim hourglass is run.

This is the room, but this is not the girl
Who looked out, fascinated then, to see
October flaunt her patterns in a whirl
Of maple leaves torn from a flaming tree.
I am a stranger here, where nothing strange
Save my reflection mirrors the shape of change.

—ELEANOR ALLETTA CHAFFEE

October Planting

His seeding done, beside his drill
He watched the clouds begin to sow
Another crop upon the hill,
The cold, infertile seeds of snow.
He wished that he could sow his grain
With such precision everywhere;
Remembered, too, how long in vain
The human hand had striven there.
He thought how earth's peculiar needs
Made every sterile flake a friend,
For always gold and silver seeds
Would come together in the end,
The harvest kernel break apart
To golden husk and silver heart.

—EVA WILLES WANGSGAARD

I Could Forget the Wind

Nothing so final now as this slow sound
Of gold, wind-shaken pears onto the ground,
Letting the boughs swing up, their harvest done
Beneath the prideful eye of Autumn's sun.

I could forget the wind that tries the door,
Fingers of firelight polishing the floor,
The first lone snowflake pausing in mid-air,
Deciding where to fall, and falling there,

But not this muffled sound of fruit that falls;
Too poignant is the memory this sound recalls,
Stabbing the silence when I would have peace
To give my Autumn-stricken heart release.

—DANIEL WHITEHEAD HICKY

October Night

It is a hunter's moon tonight,
. . . run, fox, run . . .
no shelter here and none in sight,
. . . run, fox, run . . .
that brittle disc should light you home
to pups and vixen, yet you roam
the valley, while the hunters come;
. . . run, fox, run . . .

This is the night of horn and hound,
. . . run, fox, run . . .
they wait below for scent or sound,
. . . run, fox, run . . .
here, where the white moon overhead
draws window crosses on my bed,
a chill creeps, not October-bred;
. . . run, fox, run . . .

—ADELL WEST CASHDAN

81

November

November is a symphony of grays:
The bark of trees—unnoticed during green
Leaved months and gypsy gold-and-scarlet days—
In all its patterned loveliness is seen.
The sky and lakes have taken gray for blue,
The birds conversing softly in the hedges
Were dark-gray velvet-feathered, when they flew,
And rabbits, venturing along the edges
Of gardens quite abandoned, changed their coats
Mysteriously when summer waved good-bye.
Now more than ever where its spiral floats
Upward is smoke blue-gray against the sky,
And when wind passes, whistling low or high,
Grays blending into silver seem its notes!

—ELAINE V. EMANS

Modern Thanksgiving

This is the day when I deplore
Modern science and all its lore,
Chromium trim and hooks and racks,
Rainbow pottery in gleaming stacks.
Disorder should reign on such a day:
Bowls and platters in disarray,
Spoons to lick, and pantry shelves
Piled with goodies for prying elves;
Crocks of cookies, a stove that sends
Into the kitchen savory blends;
Curtains billowing, pumpkin pies
Cooling on sills, and prying eyes
Peering to ferret out each reason
For all the specialties of the season.

But here routine now governs all:
The electric clock lets minutes fall
Precise and ordered; a button turns,
And nothing ever scorches or burns.
A switch flips low, and a switch flips high,
Mixers revolve and griddles fry.
Electric gadgets do every chore—
What busy housewife could wish for more?
I could—for I remember well
Grandmother's kitchen, its marvelous smell.
Children, forgive me for robbing you
Of the kind of Thanksgiving that once I knew.

—FRANCES RODMAN

After Frost

Frost has been here, frost has furled
The green sails on the pumpkin vine
And left the pumpkins bare; they shine
With golden Summer they drank up.
A cricket, in the vermilion cup
Of the tomato which he hollowed,
Numbed inebriate, has discovered
He has drunk his death in frost.
Bowed sunflowers look for their lost
Jet beads on the powdery ground.
All square and polished, varnished, round
Seeds shine with light of another year.
Fear grips the grasshoppers, and fear
Has brought the blood to maple leaves.
The pollen-dusted bumblebees
Have grown suddenly aware—
Death is in the crystal air.

How goes it, Everyman, with you,
Now frost washes the world in blue,
Now on the green world, woods entire
Burn with the final, farewell fire?

—ROBERT P. TRISTRAM COFFIN

84

Comfort

Day by day the leaves sift—day by day
They pass away.

I have seen joys go South, and memories blow,
And I feared winter; but I also know
I later saw white beauty from a sleigh
And moonlight on the snow.

—ROSALIE MOORE

Remember These

Remember leaves strewn on a valley floor
And sumac signals on a windy hill,
And trees that stand atremble as a chill
Wind sends a coded message on before.
The asters' last stand, brave against the frost,
A blackbird covey etched on amethyst,
Wild geese that fly to keep an ancient tryst,
And maple gold late-minded and late-lost.
Remember, too, the bittersweet that bled
Against the vine, and fields of corn grown tall . . .
The heart that holds such memories in thrall
Paints beauty on a sky as gray as lead.

—INEZ CLARK THORSON

The Warning

Now the first dim threat of autumn cleaves the air
Bringing a crispness of sunlight and fragrance of leaves.
It is less than a threat, a hand lightly laid on the hair,
But the swallow is startled, and the cuckoo believes.

Summer will soon regain the threshold of morning,
And the air and the grass and the hour grow lush and warm,
But the crickets and katydids will remember the silver warning,
And gather their trinkets in before the storm.

—MAE WINKLER GOODMAN

Philosophy for Mothers

When he grows up, I don't think he'll recall
How, on a sapphire morning in the fall,
Dust pussies tumbled up and down the stair,
And smudges lined the woodwork here and there,
While he and I ran hand in hand together,
Carefree, into the bright October weather.

I hope my son looks back upon today
And sees a mother who had time to play
Whether the work was done, or it was not;
Who realized chores are sometimes best forgot.
There will be years for cleaning house and cooking,
But little boys grow up when we're not looking.

—BARBARA OVERTON CHRISTIE

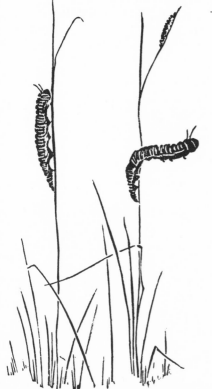

Winter

A Farm Wife at Her Window

I'm glad the first snow's come.
The bare fields look so naked in late fall!
I'm glad—although it means that winter's really here.
For first snow weaves a warm and fleecy shawl
To cover up the tired, old, brown land
So it can sleep in comfort and content
Through resting months—until March winds and sun
Take off this shawl—a soiled and cast-off garment.
Then grass and trees and flowers will start to grow.
But that's another season. Now the first snow falls
In flakes like big white stars from out the dark gray sky;
Ice shrouds the brook, stilling its rushing flow;
Even the crow's shrill voice no longer calls.
A clean hushed peace enfolds our home, like evensong;
I'm glad the first snow's come.

—LUCY MARGARET CLAPP

To Make It Home—a Fireplace

A hearth-warming, glowing fire within
Is my home's own symphony:
A melody set to a windy violin
Outside in a bare-boughed tree;

    A gay grace note in curls of smoke
    Against the laughter of merry folk;
    A crackling, soaring obligato
    To snowy popcorn's crisp staccato;

Harmonious chords, timed by the beat
Of home-leaning hearts in deep content—
That's the song of the fire, warm and sweet,
Wordless, but eloquent.

—ANNE BRADLEY

Winter in the Country

The trees, along the fences,
Join hands in muffs of snow,
And shrug their ermine shoulders
To shower me below.

 —THELMA IRELAND

Snow Sampler

Brown fields are canvas where the snow's caprice
Executes a sewing masterpiece.

Fine shirrings ripple on the cornstalk rows,
And ruffles gather where the hedges froze;
A quilting hoop surrounds the shining pond
Befringed with shadow-work of leaf and frond;
Exquisite scallops mark the tiny vales,
Cross-stitching indicates a fence of rails,
A long tree dons a needle-pointed wreath,
With rabbit tracks embroidered underneath.

How varied is the pattern and the form
Of winter samplers sewed by sleet and storm!

 —LENORE EVERSOLE FISHER

Infinitude

Within this narrow circle where we stand
Is timelessness and all infinity,
Where we see whiteness touching our own land
And glory shining on each shrub and tree.

We speak no words, nor need to speak them now,
Because it seems the very silence sings
And hymns are sounding from white grass and bough,
And through the hills the harp of David rings.

Here is the earth's most near-to-heaven mood,
This mystic, psalm-filled, prayerful interlude!

—ANOBEL ARMOUR

Mother Nature Reconverting

She's spreading soft, white sheets
Over hill and plain,
To keep her earth-bed warm
Till Springtime comes again.

She's draping barren trees
With lacy counterpanes.
And putting lids on lakes
She filled with fresh, sweet rains.

She sings some gay, wild tunes—
Keeping herself aloof—
While stringing pearls, and sewing
Fringe around the roof.

—IRENE GURLEY

Winter Painting

Bare trees along the river's edge
   Are full of charm today,
As I stand in my window here
   And look across the way.

They're sort of black—and sort of brown
   There are shades of purple, too,
With here and there an evergreen
   And white banks showing through.

Although we tire of storms sometimes,
   And gray and gloomy skies,
At painting pictures, we'll admit
   That Winter takes first prize.

—LUCY HOUGHTON JEWETT

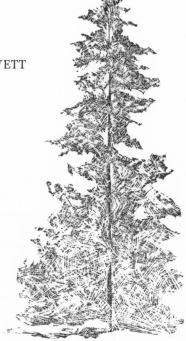

For the Long Night

The little houses on the farms bed down
In winter now, white straw of winter; snow
In forkfuls out of Heaven's loft. They know
When autumn turns the boldest hilltops brown
Then it is time to guard against the blow
Of north winds snapping, whipping; and they sink
Their stone foundations; fasten roofs, and shrink
Into their coverlet . . . A pleasant glow
Runs through them—warmth from light and fire
Behind their windows, as if someone lit
A lantern in a great barn, polished it,
The globe and burner, turned its wick up higher.

—HELEN HARRINGTON

Gift Package

The driving wind whirls from field and lane,
Clearing the way for washing, slanting rain.
And each bare limb, each bush's new-cleaned plume,
Awaits the crisping brush of frost's gray broom.
Snow then wraps earth in silver tissue sheath,
Embossed with scrollings of the shrubs beneath;
And Winter, binding it with blue-ice string,
Inscribes it: "Do not open till next Spring."

—ILA R. MONDAY

Orchard under Ice

An ice storm left the orchard silver-spindled:
Bare trees have turned to luminous glass,
Branches cracking and on fire, kindled
By the bright, cold sun. The withered grass
Is now crystal excelsior, a treasure
Packing in rhinestone brilliance a fabulous day,
And the captured heart finds in itself no measure
Of experience to compare, no words to convey
Its awareness of a beauty past believing.
One might call it some heavenly indulgence
That blessed the hard brown bones of earthly grieving,
And jeweled them with this divine effulgence.

—LUCILLE JONES STREACKER

January Snow

The heart leans on its silence,
And God, with a gentle hand
Writes with the chalk of winter
On the blackboard of the land.

—ALMA ROBISON HIGBEE

Radiant Morning

Night and the North and Boreas conspired
To bring about an alabaster world;
Now hill and tree and house-top have acquired
Resplendence where the sun's first rays are hurled
Backward to leap and crackle; from the hedge
Snowbirds fling upward with the keen wind's shift
And settle feeding near the cornfield's edge.
The frosty tinkles of their small cries drift
Back to my ears; the fortitude of tree
Bare to the wind's lash and the jagged cold;
The field's composure and the sheltered lee
Where drowse blue shadows: Beauty manifold
Invests the heart with patience to await
April's warm, certain hand at winter's gate.

—LORA D. REITER

Lonely Farm

The whirling snow, like huge, white petals blown
From heaven's tree, lay piled on fence and road.
The house was old and gray, and all alone,
And past it, storm-winds, roaring hoarsely, strode.

The fields were harvested, and now lay bare.
It seemed a wild, deserted place to me,
That windy evening through the frosted air,
A sad old house beneath a leafless tree.
But, when I entered—what a change I found!

The farmer sat within a clean, warm room,
A rugged man whom summer days had browned.
In catalogues, he read when plants would bloom,
And talked of fertile fields, of sun and seed,
And all the hungry that his land could feed.

—LOIS KINGSLEY PELTON

Snowscape with Figures

No winter-sharpened stars shine above us.
This is a night of snowfall and the black
Thick darkness crowding myriads of trees.
No sound awakes the silence but the crack
Of hemlocks when they shift a feathered hood,
And soon their music through the ice-thin air
Drifts into quiet until another branch
Curves downward, spills its mass, and swings up bare.

But other stars are in the forest's reaches,
Where little furry and half-frightened things
Search through the crystal night for sustenance,
And stars glow in the branches where trembling wings
Quietly fold themselves into the dark.
Through all the woods, down every path I go,
Small, wary eyes are watchful in the night
Like secret stars beneath the falling snow.

—DANIEL WHITEHEAD HICKY

Blue Jay in Winter

Of course he is a thief—yet he is fair.
Look at that tail shape, white bars on the blue;
See the wing markings as he pauses there
Surveying prospects far as eyes can view.

I know he is a robber, low and mean,
A coward if you will—I've seen his path:
A streak of blue straight from a raiding scene,
Before a mother robin's righteous wrath.

But see the splendor of him—not his size
Alone, but in the way he holds his head;
As though he were a king profound and wise,
Sadly misunderstood, to justice wed.

Say what you will—he is a streak of sky
Salvaged from April as he flashes by.

—ALMA ROBERTS GIORDAN

February Evening

The wind is whirling plumes of snowy feathers
   at the door . . .
(But there's shelter at the hearthfire; there is homey mirth,
   and more).

Tall, frosted trees are tinkling a million songs tonight . . .
(As the darting flames crackle, staccato sharp and light).

A far-off moon is draping silver ribbons on the pane . . .
(While shaggy logs tumble, scattering sparks
   of copper rain).

The straggling fence on the highway patterns the flat,
   white land . . .
(Inside, the warmth of sharing . . . where still, small
   strengths are fanned).

There is shelter by the hearthfire; there is homey mirth,
   and more . . .
For faith is quickened here, and here a child's bright
   dream can soar.

—PEARL LEITA PATTERSON

Snow at Dusk

Beyond the fence, where winter-purple grapes
Forlornly cluster on an ermine vine,
Wind-flurried snow whirls swiftly, settles, shapes
Long rows of drifts in shadowy design.
On ridge and hillside, bushes crouch, white-furred.
Bare branches crackle, and sere brown leaves flow
Into dim hollows where they huddle, stirred
Only by fox feet moccasined with snow.

—CHRISTIE JEFFRIES

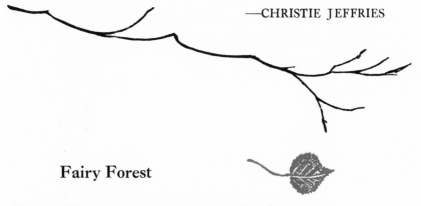

Fairy Forest

The small wood is a gleaming fairy-forest
Inhabited by Snow and brisk, young Frost;
The night-wind turns the icicles to wind-bells,
And surely all the dreams that have been lost
Lie hidden in this white, enchanted realm.
A man is wise who visits this silver wood
And losing his heart to beauty, finds himself,
And takes home from this moonlit solitude
At least one dream; one memory to keep
Of snow-like drifts of stars piled bright and deep.

—PAULINE HAVARD

February Dream

Last night I dreamed
I walked beneath the frozen earth,
Amid the roots of sleeping
Flowers and trees,
And felt these
Ice-bound prisoners stir,
Breaking the silences of their dark tomb
With faint, sweet murmurings of birth.
Within the soil's deep womb,
I heard them sigh,
Like children on the verge of waking.
Each was intent upon the task of breaking
The shell that bound it to the clay.
Each root, each seed, each bulb
Awaited, restlessly,
The faint, sure call of Nature
That would set them free.
And this I learned,
In earth's dark tunnelway:
Though singing streams are stilled
And hills are cloaked in white,
There soon will be an end
To winter's long, cold night. . . .
Spring is not very far away!

—MYRTLE VORST SHEPPARD

Day for Snow-lovers

This is a day primarily for us
Who love the snow for snow's sake—in the air,
Upon the cedars in luxurious
Pompon effect; and whitely everywhere
We step into a weightless depth of it.
No watching it through a window substitutes
For revelling within so exquisite
And pure a stuff; this is a day for boots
And Mackinaws, and energy to sally
Beyond the dooryards of us who adore
The fluff of snow in some enchanted valley,
The carpet of it upon a forest floor,
The sweep of it along a hill, and then
The curve of snow on rooftree, home again!

—ELAINE V. EMANS

December

This is the silver month of the year—
Silver-veined each oak leaf dangles;
Roofs are shingled with silver frost
And silver snowflake-spangles.
Even the stars that in summer were gold
Are fashioned of silver now,
And the tarnished silver clouds are turned
By the moon's bright silver plow.

—MARION DOYLE

Winter Haven

How good to close a door and shut out cold,
And snow, and winds that cut like unseen knives;
The skies are dark, the year is dour and old,
And grouse and pheasant lead precarious lives.

Set match to wood, and watch the red flames leap,
Set match to wick, and greet the kindly light;
Deep in a hollow tree the squirrels sleep,
Not even rabbits venture out tonight.

That other world, the work-world which I fled,
It seems so far when snows lie all about.
What need of words, as safe and comforted,
I draw the shades and shut the darkness out.

—LALIA MITCHELL THORNTON

Winter: Christmas and New Year

Star to Guide Us

I have been encountering stars everywhere for years;
Not only heavenly stars of joy and glory,
But leaf-stars that flicker in sweetgum trees,
White snow-stars tingling a child's plump palm,
Pale stars in the centers of violets, star-accented lilies.
Roses borne in star-shaped calyxes,
And stars in the centers of apples I cut and peel.
The star that is symbol of Christmas is central to life,
For He who sent the Christmas star to guide wise men
Wove through His whole creation the mark of His caring
That men should live in love for Him
And in peace and good will for one another.
He has cared forever, and forever He gives us
A star to guide us in the ways of peace.

—JANE MERCHANT

Four-year-old Angel
(Sunday School Pageant)

She seems to wear a halo. Light
Shines through her every thought tonight.
More than the Christmas carols start
The starlit music in her heart.
The shining wonder of it all,
A Babe so pink and sweet and small!
What matter then her slipping wing?
Hark! The herald angels sing!

—GERALDINE ROSS

Thought for Christmas

Softly, how softly Christmas
Lies upon the hill.
Ah, see, a star stands still
Above our very barn!
'Twas much like this the night
The Christ Child brought the shining
Light to Bethlehem.
It might have happened
Here on our own hill,
Here in our stable, warm and still.
For no man's house or barn has ever been
Too humble for the Son of God to enter in!

—MYRTLE VORST SHEPPARD

On Christmas Eve

For every child that, laughing, trims
A tree, another cries
In hunger in some far-off place,
With lost, bewildered eyes.

We talk of the Manger and the Star:
Let love, for which they stand,
Possess the heart of every one
Though strange of creed and land.

Then only will our children's joy
Not be a mockery,
And Christmas be the season's hope,
As it was meant to be.

                —PAULINE HAVARD

The Heedless Ones

If we in Bethlehem that night,
Who sheltered at the Inn,
Had slept less soundly we had heard
The heavenly host begin.

Still one of us turned restlessly—
Unduly light it seemed—
And sighed, "What is that radiance?"
And turned again, and dreamed.

While all the bells in heaven rang,
And glory shone about,
We idly drew the curtains close
To shut the Starlight out.

—FRANCES ELEONORE SCHLUNEGER

Prayer at Christmas

This is the night, Lord, of the Child, but oh
Our hearts are sad that many children need
The gifts we have no power to bestow;
The food on which their hungry mouths should feed.

God, sweep the clouds of earth away and keep
Christmas the shining thing it still should be.
In spite of grief let little children sleep
To waken in the morning joyously;

May no child lose the rapture and surprise
Entirely . . . Dear God, at any cost
Keep something of the star-shine in their eyes,
Lest all the values of the world be lost.

—GRACE NOLL CROWELL

Thoughts on a Plastic Tree

I think that I shall never see
A place to store our Christmas tree,
A tree that robs me of elation
(Where fit it in for hibernation?)
A vinyl tree for the Christmas season
Can offer not one valid reason
To be around the house at all
In spring or summer or in fall.
A tree that may at those times wear
My patience thin—for it's still there!
Phonies are bought by fools like me,
But only God should make a tree.

—MARCELENE BELL

Discovery

It seemed the usual Christmas Eve to her.
(At age sixteen the wish for something new
Is part of growing up.) She liked the stir
Of course, the bundles with shape-giving clue,
The customary wreaths with crimson bow,
Festoons of tinsel on a fragrant tree,
Familiar hearthlight and the candle glow—
Each year the same. How could she then foresee
A custom ages old could ever bring
Such sweet discovery and make this day
Star-touched for all her life's remembering?
But mistletoe has always shown the way—
That night her young heart knew a boy's shy kiss
And rose, enchanted, from its chrysalis.

—PEARL PATTERSON JOHNSON

The Star

"Rejoice!" the heavens said, "Rejoice!"
And made one star a silver voice,
So radiant against the night
A whole world harkened to its light!
Soon, an angel host would sing,
"Glory! To the new-born King!"
But the first, the purest word
Glittered so the ages heard,
The Everlasting Light was there,
Shining in the holy air.

—GERRY CARR

Christmas in the Southwest

How strange it is—a Christmas without snow
Or red-cheeked Santas stamping to keep warm
On corners sliced by wind of a winter storm.
No breath is visible; yet breezes blow
The fans of palms, their tinsel-trimmings flow,
Sparked into rainbows by the streaming sun.
Unmuffled, bootless children romp and run
Around green cactus decked with balls aglow.
Here, warm winds toss the tumbleweed, while sand
Sifts down the streets and arroyos ceaselessly,
Rippling, changing the contours of the land,
Where any moment one expects to see
Plodding on camels, eastward, a small band
Of Wise Men, seeking the Nativity.

—JEAN CARPENTER MERGARD

Small Boy at Christmas

The calendar has dwindled till at last
The months have shortened to a week, a day,
And all the dreams he hoarded in the past
Will be reality a few brief hours away.
He squirms in bed, and pushes sleep aside
To savor longer the sweet expectancy
Of what the day will bring. Dark eyes glow wide
With visions of the tinsel-laden tree.
And soon, reluctantly, his eyelids close.
The clock's hands spin around until the dawn
Will rouse him, as with sudden joy he knows
It's Christmas and the night of waiting gone.
With barefoot leaps he hurtles down the stair . . .
Then, spellbound, gazes at the wonder there.

—MAE WINKLER GOODMAN

The Little Town

Earth's towns and cities perish,
Though populous and strong.
And of them all, but one small town
Will be remembered long;
The little town of Bethlehem
That heard the angels' song.

—MILDRED GOFF

The Jar of Jelly

To others' eyes, it may not look like much;
"It's just a jar of jelly," some would say,
"Wrapped up in festive ribbons and some seals
To make it look more Christmasy and gay."
But you for whom it's meant will find, I know,
All that is packed within the little jar,
You will translate the label properly
And see just what the contents really are.
"Wild grape—" you'll say, and suddenly
You'll not be walking dusty city halls,
But down an autumn-gilded little lane
Between the jewelled vines of old stone walls.
Instead of dingy bricks beyond a court
You'll see a spruce-green hillside, sharp and clear,
Sweet fern and bayberry will scent the breeze,
The whirr of partridge wings delight your ear.
It is not much to send, this one small jar,
But you will see that in it, pure and true,
Shimmers the essence of the place we love,
Preserved especially by me, for you.

—BARBARA OVERTON CHRISTIE

118

Christmas Surprise

One of Christmas' biggest surprises
Is what friends think I wear in sizes.

—CHRISTIE JEFFRIES

Christmas Parable

The stable boy had finished work that day,
Had filled the manger with new, fragrant hay,
Had fed the beasts, and usually would sleep
Snuggled for warmth among the placid sheep;
But not tonight, for he'd conceived a plan
To join a merchant's camel caravan
And travel to far places. He had heard
Exciting tales of cities, which had stirred
His longing for adventure. He would go
Where things were happening; his friends would know
Why he had gone. He often said to them,
"Oh, nothing happens here in Bethlehem."

He looked back once, before they traveled far,
And wondered vaguely: Why that brilliant star?

—VELMA WEST SYKES

119

Universal Christmas

"Christmas is for the little ones," they say,
"Because *He* was a baby," and I wonder,
Remembering sweet Mary, why the day,
And holy Christmas Eve that blossoms under
The stars, is not for mothers? Then I see
How lonely ones, and old, and destitute,
Are best remembered then, so it must be
Their day besides. And, yearly, this is mute
And lovely evidence it is a time
For lovers: mistletoe above the door.
So, ushered in by candle-glow and the chime
Of bells, the season never can be more
For one than others now, as for the least
Shepherd of old, and Wise Men from the East.

—ELAINE V. EMANS

A Mother's Letter to Santa

Dear Santa: May I have
A private word with you?
A little confidential chat
That's just between us two?
My Johnny's sent a list of things
He wants on Christmas morn.
But, Santa, won't you please pretend
That you forgot the horn?
If you will grant this favor, please,
I'll never ask another.
Bring only toys that don't make noise,
And oblige yours truly, MOTHER.

—HELEN LEMMON

Yuletide Prayer

I pray this Christmas, Lord, for light
To see beyond the gloom of night,
For grace to grow and understand,
The warmth to lend a helpful hand,
A surer faith, a greener thumb,
The humblest heart in Christendom.

—CORINNA MARSH

Christmas Tree

The heart of Christmas is the Christmas tree—
Not just the evergreen, but all it holds.
Above the tinseled note of gaiety
Where hangs the star, a hallowed scene unfolds:
A crowded city under midnight's sky,
A swaddled Baby on a bed of straw,
A Virgin mother, Joseph standing by
While Magi kneel, like shepherds dazed with awe.

It needs but one small boy, who begs to turn
The lights to colored star-shine while he sits
Entranced by beauty, feeling beauty burn
Deep, deep inside himself—and all the bits
That twinkle on the tree blend into one
Warm flame of love—a mother's for her son.

—EVA WILLES WANGSGAARD

122

Silent Night

Time was when Christmas Eve was such a night
Of bustle, and of secret whisperings;
Of busy doings, and of parcels bright
With Christmas ribbon; with so many things
To hide from prying eyes that always kept
Close watch upon us; and the things to do
Were endless. While excited youngsters slept,
We trimmed the tree, and filled the stockings, too.
Now, with the children grown, the place is still,
The kitchen clock is heard throughout the house;
And we sit here beside the fire until
The clock strikes nine; time creeps along, we rouse
For bed, the embers crackle as we leave . . .
No house should be so still on Christmas Eve.

—VIOLET EMSLIE OSLER

Aftertime of Christmas

Small evergreen, so very brave
  In your brief finery,
Were these few days of splendor worth
  Your lifetime as a tree
Who drank of God and heard the wind
  Go singing down the sky?
The rains that knew you—and the birds
  Whose wide wings etched a high
Bright beauty on the noontime sun—
  These things will look for you . . .
Are you content? Will you have dreams
  To last your long sleep through?

—BONNIE ELIZABETH PARKER

Program Angel

Hark! A herald angel sings . . .
Cheesecloth robe, coat-hanger wings,
Halo wired above her head,
Stockinged feet for quiet tread.
"Silent night, holy night . . ."
Angelic faces shining bright,
Fourteen angels sweetly sing
"Glory to the new-born King."
I spot my angel quickly, though—
Third one right, in second row.
How could I fail to recognize
My own child's shining, star-filled eyes?

Tomorrow I will put away
The hanger wings we made today,
And pray the years may keep alight
The wonder that is hers tonight.

—JIMMIE McAULIFFE BUTCHER

Christmas Tradition

Let the children help you make
Currant cookies, Twelfth-night cake,
Anise drops and springerle,
Ginger men to trim the tree.

Share with them each ritual.
But teach them, too, the miracle
Of the Christ who came to give
Food by which the soul may live.

—DOROTHY P. ALBAUGH

Petition for a Year

Lord, you have consecrated unto us
This fresh new year, to do with as we will,
A calendar unturned, a fabulous
First page for us to fill.

There are no marks upon it; no faint stain
Dishonors this, Your gift, and, too, You give
Directions how to use it, simple, plain—
A way for us to live.

And yet, remembering how years before
Have gone, the pages exquisite
Blotched or scribbled on, I fear the more
To set my hand to it.

And I must ask You leave me not alone
With this that awes me so, must ask You stand
Beside me staunchly and, sometimes, with Your own
Firm fingers guide my hand!

                                  —HELEN HARRINGTON

A Lasting Pattern

Another year? What of it? We but grow
More certain of the good things that we know,
Less crushed by trifles and more confident
That benefits have been divinely sent.
So—"Happy New Year." May the new snow fall
On hurting things the heart should not recall,
And when the bells cease chiming and the sun
Has risen on another year begun,
May only love and faith and beauty trace
A lasting pattern on your lifted face.

—DOROTHY P. ALBAUGH

Happy New Year

Happy New Year, we say, but do
Not mean, may all your skies be blue,
All going easy, roadways straight,
And nothing come too little or late.
Happy New Year, we say, and trust
Miraculously there will just
Be right amounts of rain and bright
Weather, of sadness and delight,
Of pain and peace, of rest and task
To make the year all you would ask.

—ELAINE V. EMANS

126

INDEX TO POETS